ORIENTATION FOR CHILDREN WHO WANT TO LOVE JESUS

New Members' Orientation for Children

ALVIN C. BERNSTINE

© 2012 By Alvin C. Bernstine. All rights reserved.

Cover and Layout Design by Joyce Evans • FrootBearer Series Ministry • www.frootbearerseriesministry.com.

Published by ACB Ministry @ Bethlehem Missionary Baptist Church, 684 Juliga Woods Street, Richmond, CA 94564

Distributed by Ingram Book Group of Ingram Publications (USA) and Amazon.com

All rights reserved. NO part of this book may be reproduced, stored, in a retrievable system or transmitted in any form or by any mean – electronic, mechanical, photocopy, recording or otherwise, without prior written permission of the copyright holder, except for brief quotations in printed reviews.

ISBN: 0-9767020-2-9

FIRST EDITION

Library of Congress: Pending

This book is dedicated to all the wonderful children of Olivet Baptist Church, Mount Lebanon Baptist Church, and Bethlehem Missionary Baptist Church, who adoringly called me "Pastor".

TABLE OF CONTENTS

How to Use the Workbook 7

Introduction: God is Love 9

Lesson 1: Jesus Wants to Have a Love Relationship with You that is Real and Personal 13

Lesson 2: Jesus Sees Value in You 17

Lesson 3: Jesus is God's Gift of Love to You and The World 21

Lesson 4: Jesus Wants You to Live Life in Relationship to Him 25

Lesson 5: The Fruitful Children of Jesus, Part 1 29

Lesson 6: The Fruitful Children of Jesus, Part 2 33

Lesson 7: Living with the Jesus Family—The Church 37

Lesson 8: A Sign of Being in Jesus' Family—Baptism 41

Lesson 9: God's Love Meal for You and All The People God Loves— The Lord's Supper 45

Lesson 10: We Love by Loving One Another—Ministry 49

Lesson 11: The Church Person who Loves the People God Loves—The Pastor 53

Lesson 12: A Person Who Helps the Pastor Love the People God Loves—The Deacon 57

Lesson 13: How to Show Love to God Who Loves Us—Worship 61

WORDS FROM
Reverend Dr. Alvin C. Bernstine

Welcome to the Children's Orientation to life in Jesus and membership in His church. Over twenty-five years of serving as a Pastor, I could no longer live with the knowledge that there was a glaring scarcity of relevant material available for orientating children into the Christian family. I have seen children just tossed into the life of the church with the hope that something essential about Jesus would stick. However, it has been mine to observe that by the time many of our children reached adolescence they have formed distorted understandings of Jesus and view the church as irrelevant to their lives. At best, church becomes more of a social outlet than an experience with Jesus. Oftentimes, the church struggles to make Jesus relevant to children with its undue emphasis on ritual and religion. It is the belief of this writing that if children can better relate to Jesus they can better love Jesus.

I have tried to bring my years as a pastor of children, father, and now grandfather into producing this workbook, with the hope that it will contribute to the work of "bringing children to Jesus." Also, I have prepared this work with parents in mind, who often are lacking in direction on how to shape the lives of children who want to love Jesus.

It is my hope that this book will assist the many children who want to love Jesus in a meaningful way. I am mindful that this will only be the beginning of a life-long journey of loving the Lord, but I pray this is helpful in starting the journey. Thus, I am pleased to provide a workbook designed to assist in developing children who want to love Jesus.

I want to give special thanks to Joyce Evans, a gifted and anointed graphics artist, who has provided invaluable assistance in making this work child-friendly.

Ultimately, this book is for the many children who have loved me and have called me Pastor. Your love for Jesus has caused me to love Jesus more.

Be Blest!

HELPING CHILDREN WHO WANT TO LOVE JESUS

One of the greatest responsibilities of the followers of Jesus is the stewardship of children. Our role in shaping the lives of children is crucial to everything we do in the life of the church, moreover, as followers of Jesus. To this end, I have prepared a few lessons that I pray will assist us in handling our most precious commodity – our children.

GOAL: The primary goal of this publication is to assist in the orientation process of children who want to love Jesus.

WHY IMPORTANT: It has been our experiences that children who earnestly want to love Jesus are not adequately oriented in how to do so. Also, the parents are often ill-equipped to explain in a child-friendly manner what it means to love Jesus. As a result, many children mimic their parents, or other significant influences, and never develop a personal relationship with Jesus.

HOW TO USE

Each lesson is based upon a scripture lesson that focuses upon some facet of a personal relationship with Jesus.

Please read the scripture lesson as provided in the book.

Each lesson provides at least two suggested high points, which the teacher/parent can expound upon in a manner appropriate with the learning styles of the students/child.

Please explore the suggested high points and seek to make them applicable to the children.

HELPING CHILDREN WHO WANT TO LOVE JESUS

Each lesson provides an illustration, as well as an activity in which the children can interact with the relational focus of the lesson.

Make sure the children complete the activities, as well as interact with each other's interpretation of the respective activities.

Each lesson provides questions which reinforces the lesson's emphasis.

Allow children to answer the questions in their own way.
NOTE: Each child's relationship with Jesus is personal.

Each lesson provides an activity which requires parental/care giver interaction with the child and the lesson's emphases. (It is our belief that parents/care givers are essential to the disciple-making of children.)

Parents or care-givers are required to honestly complete the Parents and Jesus section. Please allow opportunity for the child to question, react, and respond. It is my hope that upon completion of the Orientation that you and the child will have a better sense of what it means to love Jesus.

NEW MEMBERS' ORIENTATION FOR CHILDREN

God is Love

Introduction

Lesson Goal

We want children to know God in a love relationship, for God is love.

"Everyone who loves is born of God and experiences a relationship with God. The person who refuses to love doesn't know a thing about God." (1 John 4:8)

IDEAS TO LIVE FOR:

When you love you want the same good for another that you want for yourself.

God's love is to want good for another even if you have to deny yourself.

NOTE: Unless specified otherwise, all biblical references are from the **Message: A Contemporary Translation**, by Eugene Peterson.

ACTIVITY

Love wants the same good for another that you want for yourself.

God's love is to want good for another
even if you have to deny yourself. Color the picture below.

QUESTIONS

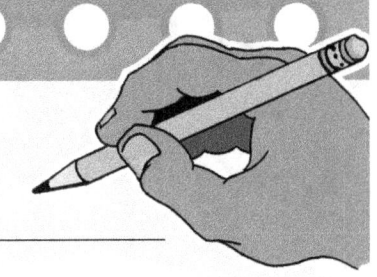

1. How do you best describe God?
   _____
   _____

2. What is love?
   _____
   _____

3. How does God love?
   _____
   _____

PRAYER

Dear God, I want to love you because I know you love me. AMEN.

PARENTS & JESUS

Give your child an example of you giving for the good of another at the sake of denying yourself.

EXTRA NOTES

NEW MEMBERS' ORIENTATION FOR CHILDREN

Jesus Wants to Have a Love Relationship with You that is Real and Personal

Lesson 1

Lesson Goal

The goal is to impress upon each child the significance of a personal relationship with God that is real.

"Let the children alone, don't prevent them from coming to me. God's kingdom is made up of people like these."

(Matthew 19:14)

IDEAS TO LIVE FOR:

Your relationship with Jesus is important to Jesus.

Jesus does not want anything or anyone to get between Him and you.

ACTIVITY

Your relationship with Jesus is important to Jesus.
Jesus does not want anything or anyone to get between Him and you. Color the picture below.

QUESTIONS

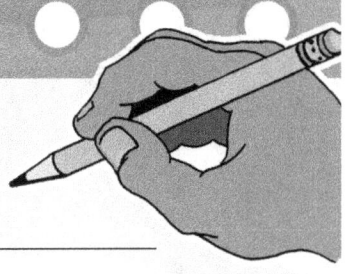

1. What does Jesus want to have with children?
   _____
   _____

2. What is important to Jesus?
   _____
   _____

3. What are some of the things and/or people that can come between you and Jesus?
   _____
   _____
   _____

PRAYER

Jesus, I want my relationship with You to be the most important thing in my life. AMEN.

PARENTS & JESUS

Give your child examples in your life where living in relationship is important.

EXTRA NOTES

NEW MEMBERS' ORIENTATION FOR CHILDREN

Lesson 2: Jesus Sees Value in You

Lesson Goal

To impress upon children that they are special in God's sight.

"At about the same time, the disciples came to Jesus asking, "Who gets the highest rank in God's kingdom?" For an answer Jesus called over a child, whom he stood in the middle of the room, and said, "I'm telling you, once and for all, that unless you return to square one and start over like children, you're not even going to look at the kingdom, let alone get in. (Matthew 18:1-2)"

IDEAS TO LIVE FOR:

You are very special in the sight of Jesus.

Jesus saw children as being the perfect examples for people who get to be a part of His special community?

ACTIVITY

Children are very special in the sight of Jesus.

Jesus saw children as being the perfect examples for people who get to be a part of His special relationship. Color the picture below.

QUESTIONS

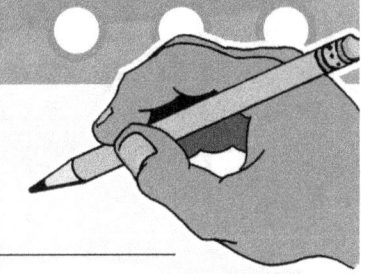

1. How did Jesus see children?
   _____
   _____

2. Who are the best models for Jesus' special community?
   _____
   _____

3. What is it about children that make them so valuable to Jesus?
   _____
   _____
   _____

PRAYER

Thank You, God, for making me special in Your sight. AMEN.

PARENTS & JESUS

Point out ways in which your child brings value to your life.

EXTRA NOTES

NEW MEMBERS' ORIENTATION FOR CHILDREN

Lesson 3: Jesus is God's Gift of Love to You and The World

Lesson Goal

To help children understand that Jesus is God's gift of love to them.

"This is how much God loved the world: He gave His Son, his one and only Son. And this is why no one needs to be destroyed; by believing in Him, any one can have a whole and lasting life. (John 3:16)."

IDEAS TO LIVE FOR:

Out of a heart of love God gave the best He had for you.

Jesus is God's gift to the world.

ACTIVITY

Out of a heart of love God gave the best He had for children.

Jesus is God's gift to the world.
Color the picture below.

Jesus loves the children around the World!

QUESTIONS

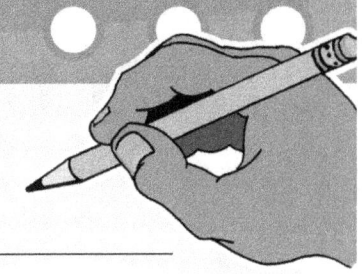

1. Why did God give His best to children?
   _____
   _____

2. Who is God's gift to the World?
   _____
   _____

3. What do children do when they receive a gift?
   _____
   _____
   _____

PRAYER

Dear God, I want to thank You for the best gift in the world—Jesus. AMEN.

PARENTS & JESUS

Demonstrate an act of unconditional love and explain the act to your child.

EXTRA NOTES

NEW MEMBERS' ORIENTATION FOR CHILDREN

Lesson 4: Jesus Wants You to Live Life in Relationship to Him

Lesson Goal

To help children understand how important it is to live in relationship with Jesus.

"Live in me. Make your home in me just as I do in you. In the same way that a branch can't bear grapes by itself but only by being joined to the vine, you can't bear fruit unless you are joined with me."

(John 15:4)

IDEAS TO LIVE FOR:

We live in Jesus and Jesus lives in us.

While joined with Jesus we are able to live fruitful lives.

ACTIVITY

We live in Jesus and Jesus lives in us.

While joined with Jesus we are able to be fruitful.
Color the picture below.

QUESTIONS

1. How do we describe our relationship with Jesus?
   _____
   _____

2. What happens when we are joined with Jesus?
   _____
   _____

3. What does a good relationship look like?
   _____
   _____
   _____

PRAYER

Wow God, I am excited about being related with You. AMEN.

PARENTS & JESUS

Show your child how you are connected to Jesus and the difference it makes in your life.

EXTRA NOTES

NEW MEMBERS' ORIENTATION FOR CHILDREN

The Fruitful Children of Jesus, Part 1

Lesson 5

Lesson Goal

To help children to understand the type of fruit that living in relationship with Jesus produces.

Love

Joy

Peace

IDEAS TO LIVE FOR:

Every fruit is about my relationship with God, myself, and others.

Every fruit is something that God gives to me to give to others.

"But the fruit of the Spirit is love, joy, peace, patience, kindness, goodness, faithfulness, gentleness and self-control. (Galatians 5:22, New International Version)"

ACTIVITY

Every fruit is about my relationship with God, myself, and others.

Every fruit is something that God gives to me to give to others. Color the children around the fruit tree.

QUESTIONS

1. How do I give my fruit to God?
   _____
   _____

2. How do I give my fruit to myself, and others?
   _____
   _____

3. What does my fruit tree look like now?
   _____
   _____
   _____

PRAYER

**God help me give to others what you have given to me.
AMEN.**

PARENTS & JESUS

Demonstrate for your child some expressions of the fruit of the Spirit in your life.

EXTRA NOTES

NEW MEMBERS' ORIENTATION FOR CHILDREN

Lesson 6

The Fruitful Children of Jesus, Part 2

Lesson Goal

To help children to understand the type of fruit that living in relationship with Jesus produces.

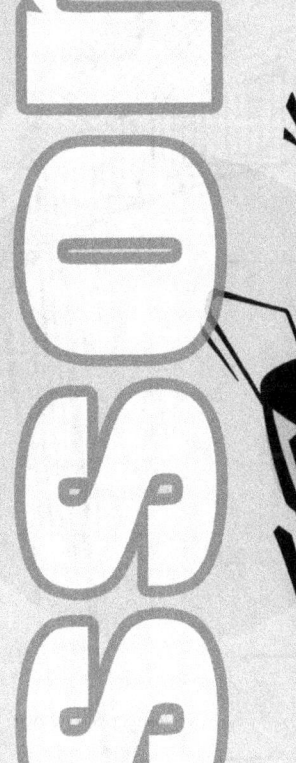

"But the fruit of the Spirit is love, joy, peace, patience, kindness, goodness, faithfulness, gentleness and self-control. (Galatians 5:22, New International Version)"

IDEAS TO LIVE FOR:

Living in Jesus is supernatural!

Every fruit is a natural expression of a supernatural relationship.

Every fruit is a gift that you give away.

ACTIVITY

Every fruit is a natural expression of a supernatural relationship.

Every fruit is a gift that I give away.
On the lines below, list the fruits of the Spirit.

1. _____
2. _____
3. _____
4. _____
5. _____
6. _____
7. _____
8. _____
9. _____

QUESTIONS

1. Why are the fruit of the Spirit natural?
   _____
   _____

2. What makes the fruit of the Spirit supernatural?
   _____
   _____

3. Who in your life can you give your fruit to?
   _____
   _____
   _____

PRAYER

Wow, God I love giving away what you have given me. AMEN.

PARENTS & JESUS

Demonstrate to your child ways in which you give away the fruit of the Spirit.

EXTRA NOTES

NEW MEMBERS' ORIENTATION FOR CHILDREN

Living with the Jesus Family—The Church

Lesson 7

Lesson Goal

To help children see the church as Jesus' family.

IDEAS TO LIVE FOR:

The church is the family of Jesus.

Jesus holds the church together by enabling people to love one another as special family members.

"And when it comes to the church, he organizes and holds it together, like a head does a body." (Colossians 1:18)

ACTIVITY

The church is the family of Jesus.

Jesus holds the church together by enabling people to love one another as family members. Color the picture below.

QUESTIONS

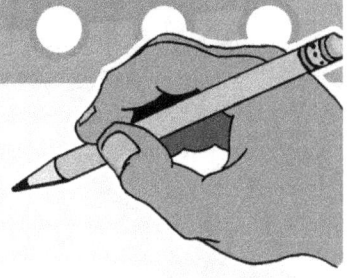

1. When we join the church we become a part of whose family?
   _____

2. How does Jesus hold the church together?
   _____
   _____

3. What kind of family member are you?
   _____
   _____
   _____

PRAYER

God, I thank you for giving me such a special family.
AMEN.

PARENTS & JESUS

Give your child examples of how church members are like family to you.

EXTRA NOTES

NEW MEMBERS' ORIENTATION FOR CHILDREN

Lesson 8: A Sign of Being in Jesus' Family—Baptism

Lesson Goal

To give children a basic understanding of baptism.

IDEAS TO LIVE FOR:

A sign of becoming like Jesus is to be baptized.

Jesus coming out of the grave was like coming out of a dark room.

A sign of belonging to Jesus' family is to be baptized.

"When we are lowered into the water, it is like the burial of Jesus; when we are raised up out of the water, it is like the resurrection of Jesus. (Romans 6:4)

ACTIVITY

A sign of becoming like Jesus is to be baptized.

A sign of belonging to Jesus' family is to be baptized. Color the picture of the baptism below.

QUESTIONS

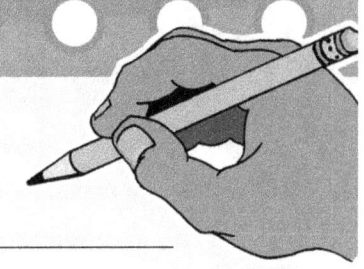

1. How is baptism a sign of being like Jesus?
   _____
   _____

2. What sign tells us that we are members of Jesus' family?
   _____
   _____

3. Why is baptism like leaving a grave?
   _____
   _____
   _____

PRAYER

Lord, I thank you for the water that makes me become just like Jesus. AMEN.

PARENTS & JESUS

Spend time showing your child that what he or she does is what identifies him or her.

EXTRA NOTES

NEW MEMBERS' ORIENTATION FOR CHILDREN

Lesson 9: God's Love Meal for You and All the People God Loves— The Lord's Supper

Lesson Goal

To teach children about the love demonstrated in the Lord's Supper.

IDEAS TO LIVE FOR:

The Lord's Supper reminds us of how much God loves us.

The Lord's Supper encourages us to love one another.

"In the course of their meal, having taken and blessed the bread, he broke it and gave it to them. Then he said, "Take, this is my body." Taking the cup, he gave it to them, thanking God, and they all drank it. He said, "This is my blood, God's new covenant, poured out for many people. (Mark 14:22-23)"

ACTIVITY

The Lord's Supper reminds us of how much God loves us.

The Lord's Supper encourages us to love one another. In the space below, draw a picture of you sharing the Lord's Supper with your family.

QUESTIONS

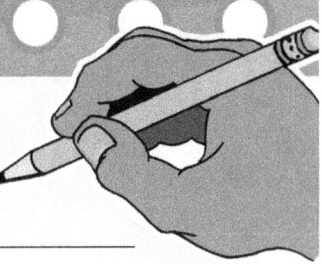

1. What does the Lord's Supper tell us about God?
   _____
   _____

2. What does the Lord Supper tell us about one another?
   _____
   _____

3. What will you remember when you take the Lord's Supper?
   _____
   _____
   _____

PRAYER

Wow, God you love me so much that you don't want me to forget. AMEN.

PARENTS & JESUS

During a family meal demonstrate what the meal tells the family about God, but also about one another.

EXTRA NOTES

NEW MEMBERS' ORIENTATION FOR CHILDREN

Lesson 10: We Love by Loving One Another—Ministry

Lesson Goal

To teach children the basic concept behind ministry/service.

IDEAS TO LIVE FOR:

Jesus expects for us to serve one another in love.

Jesus expects for us to love others the way he loved us, which is through service.

"Let me give you a new command: Love one another. In the same way I loved you, you love one another. This is how everyone will recognize that you are my disciples-when they see the love you have for each other. (John 13:34-35)

49

ACTIVITY

Jesus expects for us to serve one another in love.

Jesus expects for us to love others the way he loved us, which is through service. Color the picture below.

QUESTIONS

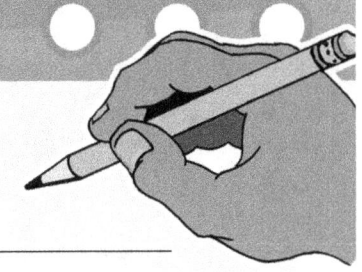

1. What is it that Jesus expects of us?
   _____
   _____

2. How did Jesus love us?
   _____
   _____

3. Give examples of ways you can show love through service?
   _____
   _____
   _____

PRAYER

**God, help me to love others the way you love me.
AMEN.**

PARENTS & JESUS

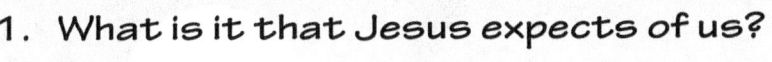

Demonstrate to your child five acts of love in service.

EXTRA NOTES

NEW MEMBERS' ORIENTATION FOR CHILDREN

Lesson 11: The Church Person Who Loves the People God Loves—The Pastor

Lesson Goal

To teach children the role of the Pastor within the life of the church.

IDEAS TO LIVE FOR:

The Pastor is a special gift from God to love the church.

The Pastor helps Christians to be better Christians.

"He handed out gifts of apostle, prophet, evangelist, and pastor-teacher to train Christians in skilled servant work, working within Christ's body, the church, until we're moving rhythmically and easily with each other." (Ephesians 4:11-12)

ACTIVITY

The Pastor is a special gift from God to love the church.

The Pastor helps Christians to be better Christians. Color the picture below of the Pastor sharing with the children.

QUESTIONS

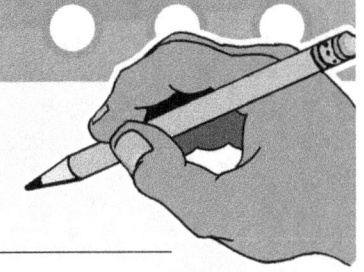

1. What is the Pastor of the church?
   _____
   _____

2. What is the Pastor's role in the church?
   _____
   _____

3. Can you name ways in which your Pastor has helped you?
   _____
   _____
   _____

PRAYER

God, I thank You for giving me a special gift in my Pastor.
AMEN.

PARENTS & JESUS

Demonstrate to your child genuine love and respect for the Pastor.

EXTRA NOTES

NEW MEMBERS' ORIENTATION FOR CHILDREN

Lesson 12

A Person Who Helps the Pastor Love the People of God—The Deacon

Lesson Goal

To help children better understand the role of the Deacon.

IDEAS TO LIVE FOR:

Deacons or Elders are to help the Pastor serve the members.

Deacons or Elders are to be good people who love God.

"It wouldn't be right for us to abandon our responsibilities for preaching and teaching the Word of God to help with the care of the poor. So, friends, choose seven men from among you whom everyone trusts, men full of the Holy Spirit and good sense, and we'll assign them this task." (Acts 6:3)

ACTIVITY

Deacons are to help the Pastor serve the members.

Deacons are to be good people who love God.
Color the picture below of the Deacon helping lead children's church.

QUESTIONS

1. Who do deacons help?
   _____
   _____

2. What kind of man makes a good deacon?
   _____
   _____

3. Can you give an example of a deacon helping the Pastor?
   _____
   _____

PRAYER

Dear God, thank You for deacons who help the pastor and teach me to love You.
AMEN.

PARENTS & JESUS

Introduce your child to a deacon of the church that he or she can love and respect.

EXTRA NOTES

NEW MEMBERS' ORIENTATION FOR CHILDREN

Lesson 13: Showing Love to God Who Loves Us—Worship

Lesson Goal

To help children see worship as an act of their love for God.

IDEAS TO LIVE FOR:

We give God our love when we worship.

Worship makes us happy people.

God enjoys our worship.

"Jesus replied: "Love the Lord your God with all your heart and with all your soul and with all your mind. (Matthew 22:37, The New International Version)"

"Worship the Lord with gladness; come before Him with joyful songs. (Psalm 100:2, The New International Version)"

ACTIVITY

We give God our love when we worship.

Worship makes us happy people.
Color the picture of the choir singing praises to God.

QUESTIONS

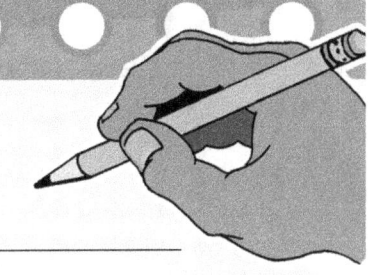

1. What do we do when we worship?
   _____
   _____

2. What does worship do for us?
   _____
   _____

3. What do you enjoy in worship?
   _____
   _____
   _____

PRAYER

**Hallelujah!
I love to worship you God.
AMEN.**

PARENTS & JESUS

Model before your child a positive worship attitude.

EXTRA NOTES

www.ingramcontent.com/pod-product-compliance
Lightning Source LLC
Chambersburg PA
CBHW051215290426
44109CB00021B/2461